Square Foot Gardening

*A Beginner's Guide to Square
Foot Gardening at Home*

Mitch Davidson

Table of Contents

Introduction

This book is for experienced planters, people who have only recently decided to start a backyard garden, and the curious. Even as a hobby, the benefits of having a flourishing garden at home are numerous. You could teach your kids the gratification of nurturing plants, instill in them a respect for biodiversity, and show them the importance of eating fresh and nutritious foods by having them assist you in the garden.

You can also save money by growing some of the food you consume, or by selling some of your produce to make extra income.

Whatever motivates you to grow and tend to a garden, you need a strategy that will not only provide order but also help your crops mature quickly and healthily. While you may have heard of numerous planting techniques to achieve an abundant, healthy, and fast yield, very few are as successful as square foot gardening for small-scale gardens.

Should you keep reading, you will gain such knowledge as which crops are most suitable in a square foot garden, and how companion planting can be incorporated to boost the results of this gardening technique. This book will not only leave you with an appreciation for square foot gardening, but provide a detailed roadmap on how to set it up and get the best results from it. So, without further ado, let's get digging!

Chapter 1: What Is Square Foot Gardening?

When compared to other traditional methods of gardening such as planting vegetables in rows straight into the soil, square foot gardening, or SFG, sets a different pace. Not only does it require significantly reduced efforts to manage and run the garden, but it also results in bumper harvests by the end of crop cycles. The reason why this system works is that the growing medium used in SFG is more manageable and lighter than traditional mediums. As such, requirements like the backbreaking work of weeding and the use of heavy gardening tools are eliminated.

Additionally, the medium used in square foot gardening only requires a relatively small area, which allows gardeners to better maintain both plant and medium. This portability ensures that gardeners are allowed ease of access from all sides of the medium to tend to their plants, allowing for better concentration and attention, which leads to healthier harvests.

Square foot gardening also involves combining complementary gardening techniques that decrease or entirely scrap the need for measures for controlling pests or boosting growth with chemicals. What makes SFG even more appealing is the inherent satisfaction that comes with the entire process of growing, harvesting, and consuming the foods you produce; and this is without taking into account that the foods produced with square foot gardening have richer textures and tastes when compared to traditionally made foods.

History of Square Foot Gardening

SFG was a concept promoted by Mel Bartholomew in the 1980s. He is responsible for coining the term and honing the craft that has since been passed down generations. The logic behind this method of gardening is simple: to grow plants devoid of toxic pollutants (fertilizers, pesticides, herbicides, etc.), as well as to save time, money, resources, and the environment at large. This logic was enough to make the concept an instant sell, with its popularity growing with time. With this widespread acceptance and fame, square foot gardening has since become ingrained in the minds of gardeners as the best way to improve plant health and production. What's even better is the promise of utilizing less space for a greater harvest.

Square foot gardening derives its name from the concept of a small frame of 4 feet by 4 feet being enough space to produce a rich variety of plants throughout a planting season. The belief is that the harvest would suffice to meet the feeding needs of a small family. The frame or box is divided into smaller square foot sections, equaling a combined planting area of sixteen square feet.

These subsections are perhaps the most important part of square foot gardening, as they are used for intensive rotational planting which forms the base of this gardening concept as a whole. When shown with the right amount of care, such a small area is capable of producing many nutrient-rich vegetables.

The idea of square foot gardening first struck Mel Bartholomew in 1975 after having been frustrated every other year by a defective gardening system. His local community garden was no stranger to wastage, and Mel was tired of seeing many good, ripe plants go to waste. To prevent such happenings from ever repeating, Mel brainstormed a more efficient system of gardening.

He was an engineer with a mind for math, so everything needed for a successful system boiled down to getting the right numbers. Mel desired a garden system that produced more rich and ripe foods in every square inch, unlike other gardening systems available at the time.

Aside from his desire for an extremely productive gardening system, Mel wanted a system that demanded less effort and energy to maintain. This addition was to counter potential inefficiencies in gardeners. For this to work, he decided on a medium that was both good-looking and self-contained – this would also remove the stress of weeding and having to use chemicals.

Mel was quite fond of the environment, and so he also wanted to create a system that was eco-friendly in and of itself. As such, the system had to use up to 90% less water than any other traditional row gardening system around. Mel was a well-rounded gardener who loved the fun of working on a garden; however, he hated the repetitive and demanding labor that came with incompetent gardening systems. Thus, he got to work on a system that captured only the joys of gardening, and what he created was the square foot gardening system we know today.

Chapter 2: Benefits of Square Foot Gardening

After reading about the history of SFG and all that it entails in the preceding chapter, you can probably list a few advantages that this gardening method has over many others. This chapter might confirm some of your excitement about square foot gardening, and it will certainly give you more than a few reasons to begin applying the technique immediately. Here, we will take a look at the biggest advantages of square foot gardening.

Not Limited to Any Location

Square foot gardening incorporates some planting techniques that make it even more successful. One such method is raised bed gardening. This allows the planter to successfully grow their crops in any part of their garden. They are not constrained by space or soil. The gardener can set their square foot garden even on cement ground.

No Heavy Equipment Needed

Planting with SFG can be done without any of the heavy machinery and equipment that is usually required for other traditional gardening methods. This also means that you do not have to worry about the storage and maintenance of such tools.

Requires Relatively Little Effort

This is one of the major selling points of square foot gardening. Since the method requires a small space to be implemented, the crops can be easily managed from seed stage to full maturity.

It is commonly said that with SFG, the same amount of crops can be grown in only 20% of the space that row planting would require. This further allows the gardener to tend to every crop without overly exerting themselves.

In addition to this, the process of digging in the earth to plant seeds or seedlings is completely eliminated with square foot gardening. By creating a raised bed, the planter can ensure fertility.

Encourages Biodiversity

As a result of companion planting that is also introduced into SFG, such gardens allow the flourishing of various beneficial single and multicellular organisms. Gardeners can exploit the fact that certain crops are able to attract the natural predators of pests that could harm more vulnerable plants.

Less Wasted Resources

In a small and more manageable space, one is able to administer water, fertilizers, and other resources more optimally and judiciously. This is not the same with row planting and other traditional styles where a greater percentage of water is lost to the earth and only very little is enjoyed by the plant.

Beginners Find It Easy

Even if you have no experience as a gardener, you can quickly get information concerning how to build a square foot garden and the right practices to get the best results. Afterward, you can immediately proceed to build your garden. There are no complicated hydroponic systems or strenuous row planting methods you're expected to know.

Little to No Weeding

Most square foot gardeners enjoy weedless planting for the first season. However, weeds are easily managed even when they appear. The planter can walk around the raised bed and pull the weeds by hand or cut them with scissors.

Crop Rotation Is Made Easy

This strategy encourages planters to cultivate different crops on the same piece of land. This is done to curb plant diseases and improve the health of the soil. Since soil isn't a major feature in SFG, crop rotation is mainly applied to deter pests and maintain the good health of crops.

As a result of the arrangement of square foot gardening, it's easy for planters to rotate the crops in each bed.

Better Use of Space

If you do any kind of research about square foot gardening, one of the first things you will find is the comparison of SFG to row planting. Praise is often showered on SFG for how well it utilizes small spaces while still producing high yields. The space between rows in traditional planting can be used to grow more crops, and square foot gardening does this well.

Quick Set-Up

Building your square foot garden does not require vast years of experience, an abundance of financial resources, nor complicated farm tools. In the next chapter, we will delve into the materials needed to set up this gardening method and the ways to go about it.

You might be excited to know that it only takes a few hours of your day to completely build your own square foot garden.

Healthy Soil

Those who choose the more common gardening methods that involve tilling the earth must work to prepare the soil so as to make it fertile for use. As you might be able to tell, this can be an especially strenuous and expensive endeavor. Maybe the most disadvantageous part of this traditional process is the time that is wasted.

Square foot gardens begin with organic matter and the healthiest soil. This not only solves the problem of exertion, but also ensures that the square foot gardener enjoys more immediate yields.

Soil Compaction Is Eliminated

Although not literally, the soil needs to breathe to remain cultivable. However, this "breathing" can become impeded as humans and animals frequently walk on a piece of land. The transportation of water and air is adversely affected as the soil becomes increasingly less porous.

Now, this can be useful if you are attempting to create a path. Otherwise, you want your garden to be structured such that the chances of the soil being compacted is reduced.

Square foot gardens, in most cases, completely eliminate such eventuality. As a result of the raised bed technique, neither you, the gardener, nor anyone else could unintentionally walk in the garden.

Chapter 3: How to Build a Square Foot Garden

To create an effective square foot garden, there are certain features that need to be taken into consideration. These features are important to the success and continuity of the system, affecting the growth and development of plants throughout the growing cycle. Let's consider these seven features:

1. Location and positioning: These are perhaps the most important considerations of the lot. A square foot garden focuses on a system that is plant-intensive. Hence, the maximization of a small land area is the main goal. To begin creating your garden, you need a good location. In that spot, you should prioritize the areas that receive good amounts of sunlight for about six to eight hours daily. It's important to observe the location from sunup to sundown to determine the prime areas.

Create your square foot garden away from shrubs and trees to avoid interference from roots and blockage of sunlight. Additionally, the location should be an area with proper drainage to avoid rainfall collecting and swamping the area.

2. Materials for creating the box: The best material for creating the SFG box(es) is untreated lumber. While it's rougher in comparison to its treated counterpart, it comes without the chemicals that can leach into the soil and affect the plants. Furthermore, make plans to create boxes with a depth of about six to eight inches. Boards measuring 2x6 or 1x6 are preferable choices.

With a power drill, some screws (deck-type), and a screwdriver, you can easily put the boxes together. If your location is grassy, you might want to lay out some landscape cloth, cardboard, or tarpaulin. Doing this will ensure the grasses and other weeds don't sprout up within the system and compete with your plants.

3. Layout and design: The number of boxes doesn't matter in square foot gardening. You can begin with one or several boxes at once. If you choose the latter, arrange the boxes in squares rather than rows. This concept extends beyond individual boxes to the entire layout. Doing this ensures better efficiency in processes like watering, weeding, and planting.

Also, create paths between the boxes that are wide enough for walking and stooping to tend to plants. The boxes can be about two, three, or four feet apart. Four feet is the maximum reachable distance. Otherwise, it will be more difficult to get to the plants.

4. Creating your soil medium: For square foot gardening to work, the soil must be rich, nutritious, and loose enough to allow for proper aeration and water absorbency. The usual soil found in your backyard won't cut it.

As a rule of thumb, you can create a good soil medium by combining one-third coarse vermiculite, one-third peat moss, and one-third heavy compost. While you are at it, ensure that your choice of compost is the true, dark variety. You can try making your own compost instead of settling for commercially-made mixes.

5. Using a grid: You can't begin planting at random in the boxes, so a grid is needed that fits on them. It is necessary for separating plants effectively and making efficient plans regarding how to make the most of the room you have in your square foot garden. The grid lines will help split the box into several equal square feet.

Creating a grid isn't that difficult. It can be created from thin plastic or scrap wood nailed evenly together. Alternatively, you can use heavy-duty strings tied across the box and hanging from nails driven into the edges of the box(es).

6. Plant choice: Just about any plant can be grown in a square foot garden. However, herbs and vegetables are the usual go-to for many gardeners. Besides, the system is designed to improve product yield. So, get the seeds of your choice and plant them in the box according to the directions for seed spacing found on the container.

If the directions advise to plant the seeds 12 inches apart, plant one seed per square. Alternatively, if the spacing is six inches, plant four seeds in a square. A three-inch spacing implies that 16 seeds can be planted in a square. Afterward, refrain from compacting the soil into the seed holes. Instead, leave it shallow, cover it with loose soil, and water it immediately.

7. Caring for the square foot garden: Unlike traditional gardening systems, square foot gardens require regular watering to run efficiently. The watering cycle varies according to which plants you're growing. However, certain watering requirements are a norm, like more regular watering during dry spells or hot summers, and watering with lukewarm water in the spring to help increase the temperature of the soil slightly.

Also, if you harvest a plant early in the growing cycle, you can plant another crop, such as June peas, for example, in the square. To avoid disrupting the growing cycle, add more compost and replace it with mid-season plants such as winter cauliflower or turnips.

Constructing the Square Foot Garden

For the remainder of this chapter, we will go into detail regarding the models used to construct a square foot garden. After reading, you should have an idea of how you will go about building your efficient gardening space.

The Basic Model

This model of construction revolves around simplicity from start to finish. The material used is often timber, and the design involves a four-sided frame that is open at both the bottom and top. However, this model can be tweaked further to achieve different aims or in order to cater to several circumstances. For instance, you might want a portable square foot garden or a fixed one. Additionally, the plants you grow determines the spin you would put on your square foot garden.

Aside from timber, the other materials used in creating a basic model square foot garden includes bricks, straw bales, cinder blocks, and other things that can be used to create a barrier that holds in compost. Timber is merely one material that is needed to create the basic model of a square foot garden.

Timber

The importance of untreated timber cannot be overstated. In this form, the wood is without potential contaminants that can interfere with the compost used in the process, and the plants in general. For the basic model, timber such as oak or cedar is your best choice. However, in the absence of either, you can opt for redwood which can have a lifespan of up to 10 years.

The timber should be cut into:

- Two lengths at 6 inches x 1.5 inches x 4 feet 3 inches
- Two lengths at 6 inches x 1.5 inches x 4 feet

Other materials needed include:

- Galvanized screw-nails or regular nails for attaching the timber to posts
- Short nails or screws for strapping (optional)
- Four short posts measuring 3 x 3 x 12 inches
- A roll of baling twine or six lengths thin strapping to mark out the boxes
- 16 3-inch screws

Equipment needed:

- 1/8th drill bit
- Crosscut saw
- Small club hammer
- Measuring tape
- Cordless screwdriver or electric drill

Making the Garden Bed

There are two ways to make the frame, depending on your system of choice: a fixed garden bed or a portable one. The latter is not altogether different from the former; the only difference is that the posts share a similar depth with the sides. The recommended depth is 4 inches, as anything above this could become unmanageable. Additionally, to hold in the compost, the bed will need a base made from plywood of ½-inch thickness.

Traditional Mode of Assembly

Step 1: Start by clearing and leveling your chosen location for the square foot garden. Keep in mind that the said location must be facing north and south, and experience a minimum of seven to eight hours of direct sunshine each day; the more hours of sunlight, the better. Also, try to avoid areas with shade from buildings, shrubs, and trees when picking your spot for your SFG beds.

Step 2: Cut your timber of choice to the recommended lengths. Next, lay out the cut timber with the shorter lengths; they will serve as the sides. With the 1/8th bit, drill two pilot holes into each end of the timber. Afterward, use the cordless screwdriver to attach the posts with the screws. Upon completion, take the two longer-cut pieces of timber, and fix them together with the screws and drill to form a square. At the end of the construction, you should have a square with an internal measurement of 4x4 feet, taking into account the thickness of the timbers, given that the timbers have a thickness of 1.5 inches.

Step 3: Next, place the frame into position. With the club hammer, gently tap each corner of the post into the ground. Hammer each post an inch or two at once until all sides are firmly seated on the surface of the ground. Alternatively, you can assemble the frame one piece at a time in the given area.

Step 4: Having placed the frame in position, the next step is to measure out your grid. Then, fix any strapping material of your choice into place. Alternatively, drive some nails into the wood at the right points and hang garden twines to form equal squares.

Portable Method of Assembly

This method of assembly is similar to the traditional method. The only difference is that the corner posts and the sides have a similar depth since they aren't necessarily fixed into the ground. A piece of plywood that's a 1/2 inch to 3/4 of an inch in thickness with a 4-foot square piece is needed to cover the base. After assembling the frame, the next step is to place it on a flat surface and attach the plywood to form an open-ended bed. The plywood should be held into place with screw nails, preferably rust-resistant ones. After doing this, several holes (up to half a dozen) can be drilled into the plywood base to help with drainage.

For portable square foot gardens, it is advised that overall depth is, at most, 4 inches. Anything more than that will make the bed heavy to move. Besides, moving the bed is a two-person task as it is, so there is no need to add more unnecessary weight. In that light, you should understand that portable square gardens are not suitable for growing most root vegetables because of their relatively smaller depths. However, portable square foot gardens are perfect for growing some root crops like brassicas and beets.

Other Methods of Constructing Square Foot Gardens

Many different materials can be used to construct square foot gardens since the goal is to create a small space capable of holding compost and draining well. However, it's advisable that you steer clear of using treated timber or wood with old paint on it. Treated timber might hold aesthetic qualities that you desire in your garden, but it is a potential hazard to your crops and to consumers in general. While many might argue that treated timber could serve longer than the untreated variety (and this is true), you are taking unnecessary risks by using it.

Chapter 4: What to Grow in a Square Foot Garden

Square foot gardening is undoubtedly one of the most efficient methods of growing plants that exists. However, before you start planting, you must figure out which crops are best kept far apart and which ones complement each other when cultivated in close proximity. You also need to know which crops thrive the most in the highly fertile and well-drained soil that is characteristic of these gardens.

Though brief, this chapter should provide you with the knowledge of how to maximize your garden by showing you which crops are most suitable in square foot gardens.

A lot of the information on these gardens advises planters to grow anything with the system. However, you must understand that not every plant can survive all the factors that make up a typical square foot garden. For instance, some plants prefer soil that isn't shallow.

While square foot gardens might contain plant-growing nutrients in abundance, its shallow soil might fail at providing the kind of support that certain plants need. Brussels sprouts and broccoli, for example, have been observed to appear weak and undersized in comparison to those grown in the actual earth.

Also, if to you the most attractive aspect of SFG is how little physical labor is required, then you might want to avoid growing vining crops. These plants never seem problematic in the beginning, but as they mature, their vines start encroaching into the space of other crops, and you have to build trellises to ensure they are kept upright. Beans are a common example of vining crops that must be allowed to stretch in order to produce a good yield.

Thankfully, there are more SFG-safe crops than not. Feel free to plant onions, chard, marigold, cucumbers, kohlrabi, peppers, squash, garlic, carrots, corn, and radishes. This is by no means the full list of crops that thrive in square foot gardens. Also, if you don't mind the extra work, vining crops like peas and beans can make for great companion plants in your garden.

Chapter 5: Companion Planting

Companion planting is as old as it is beneficial and inspiring. If you are amused by the use of the word "inspiring", consider the fact that it is a gardening method that allows plants of different species to not only cohabit, but also actively ensure each other's survival. One plant's strengths are utilized to cater to the weaknesses of another.

The History of Companion Planting

While there are several variations of this technique in today's world, companion planting finds its origins in a rich and multi-cultural history. As far back as the time of the first human settlers, we have tried to grow crops of different kinds together, either for the aesthetics or to figure out how these plants might be helpful to each other's growth.

The earliest known practice of this method is found in Mesoamerica about 7,000 years ago. Although those who inhabited the region used a style of companion planting that was not as sophisticated or ambitious as what is commonplace today, the result was just as astounding. Before the Iroquois called it the "Three Sisters", Mesoamerican planters had successfully cultivated *milpa* as a way to copy the symbiotic relationship that they observed between plants in nature. Squash, corn, and beans were the companion plants that constituted the *milpa*.

The familial term that would later be used to describe this system came about because the indigenous Americans believed that neither of the crops could survive outside the trio. Each of the Three Sisters offered its own unique abilities that were crucial to the survival of the others. The bean, for instance, is a nitrogen-fixing plant. While other crops are unable to use free nitrogen as it is found in the air and soil, beans have the ability to convert this element into more usable, inorganic compounds.

The leaves of the squash plant are large and carpet the earth, making it cool and helping it retain necessary moisture. The squash leaves also prevent the growth of weeds, and the squash spikes deter pests like raccoons. Since beans are vining crops, they need a structure to support the upward growth of their vines, and corn acts as trellises that the bean vines can climb.

The Three Sisters also served as balanced diets for the native planters who cultivated them. Beans are rich in protein, corn provides the necessary carbohydrates, and squash is abundant in vitamins and minerals.

We also know that the ancient Greeks and Romans were not ignorant of the symbiotic relationship that certain plants share. They also knew the negative consequences of having, for instance, oak groves in close proximity to olives. While they may not have studied allelopathy, they knew how detrimental it was to grow walnut trees close to their vines. Companion planting would eventually filter into Britain where people like Jethro Tull would make the technique more effective by inventing the seed drill.

The continent of Asia is not left out of the far-reaching history of companion planting. Again, we cannot be certain that Chinese farmers who lived about a thousand years ago knew about the nitrogen-fixing properties of mosquito ferns, but they certainly observed how beneficial these crops were to other plants, and they utilized it.

Companion Planting and Square Foot Gardening

SFG is chosen by many gardeners because of how well it manages any given space. Various plants are made to grow side by side in a 1-foot grid. As effective as this method is at using relatively small spaces, conserving moisture, and preventing weeds from growing, one must be careful about which plants they grow in their garden. When planters start to concern themselves with how certain plants improve or deteriorate the health of nearby crops, the study of companion planting comes into play.

Tips for Companion Planting

Since there's no way to grow crops in a square foot garden without understanding and factoring in the effects of companion planting, the following tips will be useful in helping you get the most out of your garden.

1. **Grow friends together, not families:** Be certain that crops in close proximity to each other are unrelated. This helps prevent the outbreak of disease in your garden.

2. **Never plant combatants:** Combatants are plants that not only offer little or no benefits to your main crops, but that act as pests. They might compete with your plants for space or alter the soil to be unfavorable to their growth.

3. **Cultivate pesticides:** When you think about pesticides, you can probably only imagine the toxic chemicals that are used to control pests. However, one of the merits of companion planting is that you can grow crops that are poisonous or have preventive features to the pests that would harm your main crops.

4. **Cultivate herbicides:** Again, herbicides may not always mean chemical repellents. In fact, one of the benefits of companion planting is that you can do away with such chemicals and their harmful consequences. Instead, you

are encouraged to employ nature's repellents. However, you may not have much of a weed problem since you will be growing plants in a square foot garden.

5. **Think flavor improvement:** A square foot garden offers you the opportunity to adjust everything from the location of the garden to the types of soil used. But the more you learn about companion planting, the more you will realize that you can grow crops that are superior in taste to other plants of their kind. For instance, chervil can share some of their spice with radishes if grown together.

The Benefits of Companion Planting

1. **No need for trellises:** These structures that help vining plants grow neatly upwards can be time-consuming to build. Properly setting them up might also require some expertise. Instead, you can cultivate crops with tall and strong stems that the vines can climb.

2. **Invite pollinators to your garden:** Whether you are an experienced or beginner gardener, you probably know that not all insects are harmful to plants. Some are beneficial as either pollinators or to control pests. To

attract pollinators, you can plant flowers close to your main crops.

3. **The provision of shade:** Crops have different needs, and some are unable to grow healthily if they are exposed to too much sun. You can decide to build a protective shade for them, or just plant crops that successfully achieve the same purpose. The former requires a bit of work and separate expertise, while the latter can also add to the beauty of your garden and serve as food.

4. **Aesthetics:** Yes, this deserves to be listed separately. In many square foot gardens, herbs, flowering plants, and vegetables are cultivated to produce a spellbinding burst of colors. You gain much more from your garden than fruits and spices. This can be a way to add some beauty and character to your home.

The Best Companion Plants

If you are eager to know which plants would share a symbiotic relationship with the crops you intend to grow, this section should help you understand this as comprehensively as possible.

Summer Squash

If you need a plant to serve as mulch in your garden, you might want to consider summer squash. As they mature, their leaves broaden which can help inhibit the growth of weeds and ensure the soil's water retention. Squash is one of the Three Sisters, and it has a history of being a good companion to many crops.

Companion plants: Beans, corn, nasturtiums, lemon balm, oregano, and mint

Combatants: Potatoes, pumpkins, and zucchinis

Roses

The best kinds of plants to grow with roses are those that either complement them aesthetically, or that help to repel pests (or both). Since roses need a lot of sunlight to grow well, you should be careful about planting companion crops that shade too much of the sun from your roses.

Companion plants: Parsley, thyme, onions, marigolds, lavender, flowering tobacco, and catmint

Combatants: Azaleas, hibiscus, California poppies, and morning glories

Basil

This plant is often cultivated because of the beneficial insects it attracts and how well it does the job. If you also worry about the infestation of whiteflies, aphids, and mosquitoes, then cultivating basil is the right move. It is unclear if anise will improve or reduce the ability of basil to produce oil. This means that if you must plant the two as companion plants, you should be extremely observant.

Companion plants: Tomatoes, parsley, asparagus, apricots, peppers, beans, and oregano

Combatants: Sage, rue, cauliflower, and cucumbers

Onions

These can be the perfect herbicide for your square foot garden. They have a strong smell that can discourage pests from attacking your cabbages. They are best grown in soil pH of 6.0 to 6.5. They are also sun-loving plants, so ensure that they are not planted under too much shade.

Companion plants: Peppers, lettuce, broccoli, Brussels sprouts, and kale

Combatants: Peas, sage, shallots, garlic, and asparagus

Lettuce

If lettuces are not planted with other closely related vegetables, are given enough water, and protected from too much exposure from the sun, you will find them to be one of the fastest growing plants in your garden. They are annuals with bright green leaves that can bring some much-needed vibrancy to your square foot garden.

Companion plants: Radishes, marigolds, onions, beetroots, and carrots

Combatants: Peppers, aubergines, broccoli, kohlrabi, cauliflower, and tomatoes

Cabbages

Cabbages are attacked and affected by a host of pests and diseases. In growing this biennial, you may have to confront moths, aphids, flea beetles, maggots, and cabbage loopers. However, these can be easily managed by having strong-smelling herbs like dill, peppermint, hyssop, and oregano as neighbors to your cabbages. These herbs, like chamomile, can also add a kick to the taste of your cabbages.

Companion plants: Onions, chamomile, peppermint, rosemary, sage, oregano, thyme, hyssop, marigolds, celery, yarrow, dill, spearmint, and beets

Combatants: Pole beans, mustard, grapes, and strawberries

Garlic

This is one of nature's most highly effective pesticides. Onion flies, cabbage loopers, aphids, spider mites, and codling moths are kept at bay by the presence of garlic plants. Gardeners also enjoy growing it because of how little maintenance it requires. The most important factor in their development is their exposure to the full sun. Garlic is a great companion to most plants, save the few whose growth is stunted when planted close to it.

Companion plants: Broccoli, Brussels sprouts, and cabbage

Combatants: Sage, strawberries, asparagus, peas, beans, and asparagus

Tomatoes

This juicy crop, while not the sweetest of fruits, can be enjoyed without having to cook it. The tomato plant is credited for its many health benefits. These include its promotion of a healthy heart, weight loss, and healthy skin. They come in several variations of color, although the most common type is the red tomato.

Companion plants: Marigolds, carrots, parsley, nasturtiums, leaf lettuce, and chives

Combatants: Brussels sprouts, collards, potatoes, kohlrabi, and fennel

Peppers

Like tomatoes, peppers come in various colors. They are also fruits, even though we prepare them like vegetables. Their pungency can be used to discourage a number of pests from feeding on and destroying the other crops in your garden.

Companion plants: Tomatoes, eggplants, carrots, squash, geraniums, and cucumbers

Combatants: Fennel, lima beans, cabbage, mustard, broccoli, and Brussels sprouts

Dill

As a companion plant, dill is usually grown because of how well it deters pests such as ladybugs, hoverflies, honeybees, and butterflies. Gardeners are advised to avoid growing dill and carrots close together. This is because of how related they are and the possibility that diseases could arise due to cross-pollination.

Companion plants: Onions, basil, asparagus, corn, and Brussels sprouts

Combatants: Caraway, bell peppers, fennel, potatoes, and carrots

Borage

This herb can be especially beneficial as a companion plant. It can ward off small insect pests by attracting bumblebees. It has also been observed to improve the ability of nearby plants to resist certain diseases. As an added benefit, borage plants are great for inviting pollinators to your square foot garden.

Companion plants: Squash, strawberries, and tomatoes

Combatants: Onions, sage, garlic, and basil

Catnip

Catnip is often grown for felines. It is free of chemicals and healthy for them. In your garden, they can also serve as natural pesticides. Squash bugs, beetles, cockroaches, and aphids are some of the pests that are repelled by this plant.

Companion plants: Squash, pumpkins, hyssop, and beets

Combatants: Sage, oregano, and other closely related herbs

Radishes

Like carrots, radishes are root crops that are often eaten raw. Medically, these plants are a great source of Vitamin C and anthocyanins, which ensure that the heart continues to function well. They are fast producing crops that will thrive in most conditions. However, you must be careful not to allow them to be entirely shaded by tall plants.

Companion plants: Cucumbers, peas, chervil, lettuce, and melons

Combatants: Hyssop

Cauliflower

Finding good neighbors for this annual crop might require a bit of experimentation. They are considered somewhat fussy by many gardeners, but this is only to be expected of a vegetable that Mark Twain described as a "cabbage with a college education". To make sure your cauliflower is not affected by clubroot, you should perform crop rotation.

Companion plants: Celery, tomatoes, Brussels sprouts, broccoli, and chard

Combatants: Strawberries

Cucumbers

If you are considering growing this plant for the first time, take note that they require a lot of space and moisture. In fact, if you take care of your cucumbers well enough, they will take up even more space. As such, the best plants to grow as their companions are those that will tower above them and may not need as much water.

Companion plants: Radishes, beans, corn, and sunflowers

Combatants: Late potatoes and melons

Strawberries

While some plants crave the full blast of the afternoon sun, others just wilt. For strawberries, anything more than a little sunlight can be quite detrimental. This is why they thrive with companions that can provide that much needed partial shade. Strawberries must also contend with a number of pests. So, it is advised that you plant companion crops that can deter both animal and insect pests.

Companion plants: Borage, lettuce, bush beans, and spinach

Combatants: Cabbage and spinach

Marigolds

When you cultivate a plant like marigold, you do not just get colorful flowers that are all too beautiful to behold—they are also pollinators and insect predators. Marigold can help boost the development of crops like gourds, squash, tomatoes, and basil. Add this to the fact that marigolds are friendly with every crop, there is no reason not to have this resilient plant in your garden.

Companion plants: Every garden plant

Combatants: None

Spinach

This is another plant that has no real enemies. Spinach has the advantageous ability to produce saponin. This compound is able to successfully fight against many fungi and bacteria. Spinach is so rich in saponin that even nearby plants can benefit from it. Spinach plants are best grown in a soil pH of 6 to 7.5. It is also important that partial shade is provided for this vegetable.

Companion plants: Celery, cabbage, dill, strawberries, cauliflower, and eggplants

Combatants: None

Potatoes

One of the ways to figure out good companions for your potatoes is to understand the root systems of its potential companions. Potatoes grow inside the earth, and this means that their roots travel deep and wide. In choosing neighboring crops, keep in mind that they must be plants that will not compete with the roots of your potatoes. Thus, they should have shallow roots. Crops with roots that won't compete with potatoes include scallions and lettuce.

Companion plants: Onions, beans, corn, cabbage, radishes, and peas

Combatants: Turnips, sunflowers, melons, tomatoes, and squash

Corn

Remember the Three Sisters? Corn has been a staple of companion planting for as long as the method has been documented. Corn consumes nitrogen as a major part of its nutrition. As such, it is important that you plant nitrogen-fixers and other crops that enrich the soil with nitrogen as companions for it. Corn can also act as a trellis for the crops that need this structure.

Companion plants: Sunflowers, beans, squash, and cucumbers

Combatants: Celery, cabbage, and tomatoes

Nasturtiums

Nasturtiums are a great crop choice for beginner gardeners. They grow quickly, even with little involvement from the planter. But don't let the ease of planting nasturtiums make you look down on it. This crop has a very versatile use, whether as a companion plant or food. Nasturtiums are effective natural pesticides if your garden is being ravaged by aphids; they invite hoverflies that kill these pests. Nasturtiums excel in sandy, well-drained soils. You should also provide only partial shade for the plant to help it grow healthily.

Companion plants: Squash, apples, potatoes, cabbage, pumpkins, radishes, and beans

Combatants: None

Beans

As explained when we discussed the Three Sisters, beans are very beneficial as companion plants. They are nitrogen-fixing plants, and they extend the advantage of this ability to neighboring crops. This means that the right plants to grow with beans are those that are incapable of using nitrogen as it occurs naturally, and that can provide support for the vines.

Companion plants: Strawberries, carrots, beets, catnip, cucumbers, and marigold

Combatants: Shallots, fennel, onions, and garlic

Swiss Chard

If the weather is hotter than usual and you are experiencing a slight drought, this might still be a good time to cultivate Swiss chard. Unlike spinach, this plant can survive harsh conditions and still yield a good harvest. Chard can also be used as a natural mulch in your garden. Their broad leaves help the soil retain its moisture and shade smaller plants and seedlings from full sunlight.

Companion plants: Kohlrabi, bush beans, and onions

Combatants: Pole beans

Kohlrabi

This is another vegetable that grows without requiring much from the gardener. If planted in a cool season, kohlrabi is a fast-producing crop that can also act as a natural pest repellent. However, you must be careful not to plant other members of the brassica family close to it. This is because most vegetables in this family are often plagued by cabbage worms and flea beetles, and you would expose your garden to being ravaged by such pests if you group them together.

Companion plants: Broccoli, spinach, Brussels sprouts, and celery

Combatants: Tomatoes, fennel, and pole beans

Parsnips

These root vegetables love the full heat of the sun. So, make sure there are no tall or large plants nearby shading them. Parsnips are good companions for most plants. However, it is advised that you do not plant them in close proximity to the perennial larkspur. Parsnip flowers will call insect predators to your garden. Pests like aphids and red spider mites that are not deterred by insect predators will be discouraged from attacking your garden by the toxic chemicals that are released by the roots of your parsnip.

Companion plants: Wormwood, radishes, and onions

Combatants: Larkspur

Peas

For some crops to make good companions, they must share harvest time with other plants. Peas, however, can form lasting, symbiotic relationships with other plants regardless of their harvest time. Peas are also nitrogen-fixing plants, but they require some support for their tendrils. As such, you might want to plant corn with your peas. Basil and turnips help peas from being overcome by aphids and thrips.

Companion plants: Turnips, beans, potatoes, corn, radishes, carrots, and cucumbers

Combatants: Shallots, garlic, onions, and leeks

Tarragon

This plant cannot survive frost. So, you should wait until they can enjoy the full light and heat of the sun or partial shade. This perennial can grow as tall as 6 feet in height and is beneficial to every garden plant. Tarragon has a smell that is an effective deterrent to many pests.

Companion plants: Wormwood, beans, turnips, onions, radishes, leeks, cucumbers, and garlic

Combatants: None

Carrots

Do you enjoy eating carrots? What if you could improve the taste of your favorite crunchy veggie? By growing chives as their companion, you can harvest an even tastier crop of carrots. Other plants like leeks, nasturtiums, and rosemary are useful for preventing the pests that attack carrots. If you start planting your carrots as early as spring, they can keep producing even until autumn.

Companion plants: Every garden plant, but best grown with leeks, herbs, and lettuce

Combatants: None

Chapter 6: The Importance of Crop Rotation in Square Foot Gardening

While your square foot garden may not be the size of a modern farm, some techniques used by farmers still apply. One such technique is crop rotation. For your square foot garden to be successful, you need a proper system of rotation for the crops you intend to plant. Thus, as any one of the planted crops nears the end of its growing cycle, you should plant a different one in its place. Doing this will ensure that nutrient depletion is avoided.

Planting the same crops repeatedly in the same area is likely to deplete the nutrients necessary for that plant to grow. However, in planting a different crop, careful management ensures that the land remains rich in nutrients and refreshed all throughout the growing period.

Crop rotation also helps with pest control as some plants are organic repellents of both pest infestations and soil-borne diseases that may occur after the previous plant has been harvested. For further clarity, there are a couple of recommendations concerning how crops should be managed in a rotation system. These rules are based on the principles discussed below.

Bear in mind that vegetables are categorized into four main types, namely as follows:

- Fruit-bearing vegetables: These are crops planted for their fruits. Examples include watermelons, strawberries, tomatoes, pumpkins, cucumbers, peppers, sweet corn, aubergine, courgette, and squash, among others.

- Legumes: These are dicotyledonous plants grown for their seeds or fruits. Examples are broad beans, peas, french beans, and runner beans.

- Leafy greens: These are vegetables grown for their leaves. Examples include spinach, cauliflower, lettuce, cabbage, and broccoli.

- Root vegetables: These vegetables are grown for their edible roots. Examples are carrots, beetroots, leeks, radishes, onions, potatoes, rutabaga, sweet potatoes, shallots, and garlic.

Also, it's worthy to note that plants belong to several families according to the classification of organisms. For example, while the categorization may put them in different stratas, potatoes and tomatoes belong to the same taxonomic family. As such, they share similarities in the pests that affect them, and they drain the soil of the exact same nutrients. Of course, this implies that both should neither be planted next to each other nor after the other. Instead, they should be grown on separate pieces of land.

Since the main aim of proper crop management is to ensure that the nutrients in the soil aren't entirely depleted by planting the same or similar vegetables in the same space or after one another, knowing their taxonomic families becomes a priority in crop rotation.

Below are some families and the plants that fall under them:

1. Cruciferae, or the cabbage family: Plants in this family include every variety of mustard, cauliflower, cabbage, pak choi, turnip, radish, swede, and rocket.

2. Fabaceae, or the pea and bean family: Plants in this family are inclusive of but not limited to french beans, peas, broad beans, mange tout, runner beans, and borlotti beans.

3. Umbelliferae, or the carrot and root family: Crops in this family include dill, carrots, celery, parsnips, coriander, fennel, parsley, and celeriac, among others.

4. Solanaceae, or the potato and tomato family: This family includes vegetables like tomatoes, potatoes, aubergine, and peppers.

5. Chenopodiaceae, or the beetroot family: Vegetables under this category include beetroot, spinach, Swiss chard, and perpetual spinach.

6. Alliums, or the onion family: Plants in this family include every variety of onion, shallot, leek, garlic, and chive.

7. Cucurbits, or the squash and marrow family: This family comprises vegetables such as squash, melons, cucumbers, marrow, pumpkins, and courgette.

8. Other miscellaneous plant families: Other families comprise chicory, sweet corn, cress, all fruit, corn salad, Jerusalem artichoke, basil, oregano, asparagus, mint, okra, lettuce, salsify, and others.

Rules for Practicing Crop Rotation in a Square Foot Garden

1. **Roots vs. rich soil:** As counterintuitive as this might sound, root vegetables don't do particularly well in soils that are extremely rich in nutrients or that are over-fertilized. Since the aim of planting such crops is for their edible roots, the shoot system isn't a top priority here. In rich soils, the leaves and shoots will blossom at the expense of the roots, which should otherwise be prioritized. For instance, in your crop rotation, try growing parsnips after a successful growing cycle of more

nutrient-demanding crops such as brassicas which are known to break down soil richness.

2. **Legumes before brassicas:** It's a rule of thumb in crop rotation that brassicas always come after legumes. This implies that crops such as kale, cabbage, and cauliflower should only be grown in areas where plants like beans and peas were harvested. Doing this ensures that the brassicas blossom well, tapping into the nitrogen reserves fed into the soil by the leguminous plants.

Plant Management

Supporting Plants in Square Foot Gardening

Plants grow in many different ways, and some tend to need support one way or the other. This is especially so when these plants begin bearing fruits that put on weight over time, thus straining the stems.

There are several ways to create support systems for plants, although the primary go-to's in square foot gardening are garden twines, cages, and canes. Whatever the case, the logic is the same and is as easy as they come.

For instance, a typical cane and string trellis system can be used to support climbing plants such as tomatoes, peas, and beans. However, for plants with heavier fruits such as cucumbers, zucchinis, and marrows, the support system has to be one with a good load-bearing capacity. Basically, this translates to using heavier supports and thicker strings.

Other alternatives include using wire fencing materials such as the heavy farmers' 4-inch mesh to create a cage around your square foot garden. As the plants grow, they will lean against the cage or can be strung up for additional support. The wire itself is bent into shape and held in place by an even thinner wire to prevent it from coming undone. Furthermore, it is cut in such a fashion that it leaves a protruding end that can be sunk into the soil to secure the cage. While these cages tend to be self-sufficient by themselves, one or more canes can also be attached to hold them in place.

A typical trellis support system can be used to support a variety of climbing plants. The canes used bear the majority of the weight, while garden twines are locked into eye-fixings on each post to help in supporting and spreading the plants further. Such a support system can be erected at the back of your square foot garden or anywhere else, depending on your requirements. You could also choose to set up the trellis system in a wigwam fashion.

Planting Zones

In square foot gardening, timing is a key factor. However, finding the right time to plant your seedlings or seeds depends on the region in which you live, as times and seasons tend to vary across the globe. As a result, it is nearly possible to pinpoint the exact months or days for growing any specific set of plants by studying the weather. Instead, go with the local knowledge in the zone you reside in. However, there are plant hardiness zone maps for every region that can show you the plants that may or may not thrive within a given season.

Notwithstanding, there is nothing better than receiving knowledge used by the local farmers and gardeners. Thus, it is advisable that you find some information from local sources around you such as other gardeners on the internet, or garden centers and farmers' markets.

In that light, it can be easy to put zone maps out of the question, but don't do that just yet. Take into consideration the extremes of humidity, periods of frost and chill, summer weather, and other factors as shown on these maps. This information is handy because every weather condition has a significant effect on the vegetables that you plan on growing.

With that in mind, do not hesitate to look up a zone map as shown by the department of agriculture in your region. Checking out your zone will help you garner more knowledge of the plants that will thrive best and how to prepare for the weather.

Chapter 7: Common Vegetables to Grow in Your Garden

Carrots

Carrots are one of the more common types of vegetables that are consumed both raw and cooked. The preferred medium for growing them in is light, sandy soil. While carrots have an organic resistance to many diseases, they are susceptible to the dreaded pest known as the carrot fly. To protect them from these pests, it is best to plant carrots with onions and chives which help disguise the smell that attracts the flies.

How to Plant

Ensure that the soil used does not contain stones nor other obstructions which can result in the plant splitting or "forking out" over time. Plant your carrot seeds 1/2 an inch or thereabout into the soil a couple of weeks before the final frost of spring.

Thin out the plant by snipping some parts off with scissors instead of pulling them off when it grows above two inches in height. When planting in multiple areas, space the plants out about two to three inches from each other.

Caring for Carrots

Make sure to clear weeds regularly, but do so without disturbing the soil around the carrots. Any disruption can give off the smell of the plants and attract carrot flies.

Carrots get a richer flavor during the period of the first frost. As such, it's better to forgo harvesting until that time. To avoid pests, cover the soil with mulch, and leave the carrots in place until you are ready to harvest them.

Harvesting Your Carrots

Carrots are typically ready for consumption after ten weeks of planting. As mentioned earlier, they can be left in the soil for longer with protection from the frost. Alternatively, they can be uprooted, cleaned, and have the tops twisted off. Afterward, the carrots can be stored in sealed plastic bags and placed into a refrigerator, or they can be buried in moist sand until they are ready for consumption.

Sweet Corn

Sweet corn is a tasty crop that is loved by many across the world. It can be boiled in water or roasted over embers, and it's typically served hot and coated in melted butter. Sweet corn is a vegetable that thrives in warm weather. As such, it should be grown in a long season devoid of frost to reach its maximum potential.

How to Plant

Sweet corn is best grown from a seed that is placed down directly into the square foot garden. Place three seeds per square, an inch deep into the soil. Planting should be done during two to three weeks following the final frost when the temperature of the soil is about 60 degrees or more to ensure proper germination.

Place gardeners fleece over the soil to protect the seeds from cold spells going forward. Since sweet corn is pollinated by wind, planting three seeds per square creates a clump of three plants to help in this regard.

Caring for Your Corn

Sweet corn has a shallow root system, so it's imperative to water it regularly, particularly when corn heads begin to sprout.

The perfect medium for growing corn is well-drained soil with good moisture retention, so basically, the ideal soil for square foot gardening. Be careful when weeding around the plants to avoid damaging the shallow roots.

When to Harvest

The harvest time for sweet corn is simply when it's ripe. This is when the tassels on your sweet corn turn brown and the cobs are full.

Remove the fruits by pulling down the cob and twisting it away from the stem. Sweet corn tends to lose its flavor soon after harvesting, so it's best to consume it quickly. Otherwise, you have the option of freezing and storing it for later.

Beets

Beets are another staple vegetable for gardeners, especially in northern climates as they tend to thrive in much cooler environments. They make fine crops that last for long seasons and are able to adapt and survive in frosty weather. Beets grow well in areas rich in phosphorus, while a higher ratio of nitrogen will lead to smaller bulbs and extreme leafiness.

How to Plant Beets

Beet seeds should be sown one to two inches from the other, about a half-inch deep into the soil. It's important to wait until the temperature of the soil reaches 50 degrees before sowing. Should the weather allow, planting could begin sometime around the late periods of March and April, stretching all the way to late into the growing season.

Planting can also be timed across a 20-day interval to allow for a season-long growth of beets. Beets make a fine crop for even into late winter in regions that are zone 9 and higher.

Caring for Your Beets

Start thinning out the plants when they grow to around 2 inches in height by snipping them with shears or pinching them off near the base. Whatever method you choose to use, ensure that you do not disturb the soil around them. Maintain a gap of three to four inches between the seeds during planting.

Harvesting Your Beets

Beets are typically ripe for the harvest within 50 to 70 days, although they can be harvested within the period after the bulb first appears. While they can be left for longer in the soil, they will only grow tougher and develop a somewhat woody texture. The leaves are also tasty and make for a good ingredient in several salads.

Aside from storing beets in a cool and dry area, they can also be frozen, canned, or pickled which preserves them for longer.

Cabbages

Cabbages are another popular vegetable known for their multiple varieties that allow different opportunities for several taste preferences and growing conditions. They have a high iron content and thrive in cool temperatures. As such, they are best planted within early fall and spring.

How to Plant Cabbages

The planting pattern for cabbages isn't much different from that of Brussels sprouts. Start by planting the seeds indoors for around eight weeks leading to the last spring frost. Begin transplanting the cabbages into each square or your square foot garden about a fortnight before the final frost.

Caring for Cabbages

Try to keep the soil moist at all times, and be wary of cabbage butterflies which are the chief pests of the plant. Cabbages are highly susceptible to caterpillars, too, so plant it alongside other companion plants that can mask its smell or repel the pest.

Harvesting Your Cabbages

Cabbages are ready for harvesting when a desirably firm head is formed. Usually, it takes around 65 days or so for such firmness to be achieved.

Remove the cabbage heads by cutting them off at the base. However, remember to leave the stem and the outer leaves planted in the soil. Over time, the plant will grow fresh shoots to form other new heads. Leave about three to four of these heads to grow, and they will develop miniature cabbage heads.

Ensure that the cabbages are dry before coating them in plastic wrap and storing them away in a cool, dry place for a maximum of two weeks.

Brussels Sprouts

Brussels sprouts aren't like the other vegetables that are largely loved. They teeter on a love-hate scale with no in-betweeners. For some folks, Brussels sprouts are the sweetest thing since honey. For others, they are bile on the tongue. This disparity in taste boils down to the enzymes on the taste buds. If you're one of the people that loves them, they make a great addition to any garden!

How to Plant Brussels Sprouts

Start by planting the seeds indoors. Each seed should be planted two to three inches apart, about half an inch deep for around six weeks leading to the final frost of spring. Thin out the weakest of the lot, and transplant the rest into your square foot garden. Remember to plant one per square.

Caring for Your Brussels Sprouts

The upside of growing Brussels sprouts is that doing so doesn't demand regular ongoing care. Thus, as long as the required nutrients are met and your plants are watered sufficiently, there is little to nothing you will need to do but wait for the harvest.

When to Harvest

Brussels sprouts are ready for harvesting when they reach a diameter of one inch from the stalk. Store them in a cool, dry place or in a fridge for a couple of days before eating them. Also, do not attempt to wash the plant until you're ready to consume it. If kept slightly above freezing temperatures, Brussels sprouts can last for three to five weeks.

Green Beans

Green beans are a fine specimen for any kitchen and can also be consumed raw right after harvesting.

How to Plant Green Beans

Transplanting green beans isn't a good idea, so they are best grown by direct planting. Sowing should be done around the last frost of spring when soil temperatures grow to 50 degrees Fahrenheit.

The seeds should be planted three inches apart and an inch deep. Ensure that your garden has a support system like canes or a trellis to help the plant as it grows. Plant green beans two to three weeks apart if you want to have the crop all season long.

Caring for Green Beans

Green beans work well as starter crops because they are easy to cater to. Care typically involves regular weeding and watering, which should only be done on sunny days to avoid overly soaking the foliage.

How to Harvest Green Beans

Green beans should be carefully snipped from the stem before they fully develop. This will ensure they retain their best flavors and do not grow tougher.

Place them into an airtight container and store them in a refrigerator for the best results. To store them for longer, blanch the green beans before freezing them. Alternatively, you can pickle or can them.

Chapter 8: Tips for a Successful Square Foot Garden

In this chapter, we will go over twelve of the most helpful tips for making your square foot garden a complete success. If you keep these in mind as you build and maintain your garden, you can really make the most out of your space.

1. Make use of vertical spaces: Try as you may, there will almost never be enough horizontal space in a garden. However, if left unchecked, plants can grow to outcompete each other, leading to poor harvests. To avoid this, you will have to use vertical spaces.

There are a variety of ways to utilize vertical spaces, such as ladder mesh trellises and ladders, among others. Vertical spaces help with creeper plants, allowing for a tidier garden with an equal dispersal of sunlight and other resources.

2. Start on a small scale and gradually grow out: Creating a raised bed that is four feet by four feet is one of the easiest ways to start a square foot garden system. The 4x4 system is easier to build and can be used to grow a substantial number of crops for such a small area.

Beginning with one of these simple beds is manageable and helps for better learning on the fly. As your experience grows over time, you can add more beds.

3. Grow complementary plants: It's a common tradition among gardeners and farmers alike to plant companion or complementary plants together. The logic behind this concept balances on the said plants not shading each other out or being natural repellents to pests and diseases of the other.

For instance, tomatoes are common companion plants to zinnias. The chances of getting a healthier and better tomato harvest increases when planted with them.

In another instance, spinach and cucumbers are a complementary duo. When the former is ready to be harvested, the cucumbers will assume the vacuum left by the spinach. Also, growing peppers and tomatoes together is a complete no-no. Not only do they belong to the same vegetable families, but the tomatoes will grow to overshadow the peppers, leading to stunted growth from insufficient levels of sunlight. Be aware of how the different plants interact with one another before choosing where and when you will plant them in your garden.

4. Use a grid system and make plans going forward: Making plans on the positioning and layout of plants in a grid before planting is an important step in ensuring the success of your garden. Grids are easy to design, and they help to organize the layout of the garden system. Also, since everything can be visualized, it helps to plan ahead.

Doing this, you will realize potential mistakes like spacing problems, and overlapping plants. In that light, you will be able to plan against these potential headaches and achieve better yields at the end of the day.

5. Weeding and watering the garden: Recall that square foot gardens tend to have problems with water drainage because the soil is loose. Thus, they can dry out easily. For most plants, you'll need to make plans to water the beds daily, especially in the summer. However, the system is quite self-sufficient and may not always need water. Thus, ensure that you only water when necessary to prevent going overboard.

To ensure that you water your plants correctly, try feeling the soil with your fingers before watering. If it feels dry to the touch, water as needed. However, if there's a bit of moisture in it, watering may not be necessary.

Another source of worry and a constant pain for many gardeners is weeds. However, as mentioned earlier, square foot gardening clamps down on the formation of weeds, prevailing over traditional gardening systems. With a much closer planting space, there is little to no room for weeds to sprout up and compete. Albeit, this doesn't mean the system is entirely free of weeds.

Unwanted plants can be stubborn. To prevent weeds from growing, competing, and thriving with the rest of your plants, you should remove them from your beds weekly when your plants are young. As they mature, you should weed the beds when necessary.

6. Soil could be more expensive than you imagine: Square foot gardening involves making new garden beds. These beds need new, different soil mediums to succeed. Keep in mind that the cost of soil can sometimes exceed the price of setting up the garden bed by as much as two to four times. Additionally, your soil of choice has to be one with good nutrient and water retention. When setting up your garden bed, you will likely need a mix of organic materials, compost, and topsoil.

7. Take depth into account: Bear in mind that certain plants have a deeper, more extensive root system. To cope with such crops, it's important that you use beds with the proper depths. To grow such root vegetables, create your planting beds with a minimum of 12 inches of depth. The maximum ideal depth is around 18 inches.

8. Extra savings on high-raised beds: If you choose to make high-raised beds for your square foot garden, you will have to spend more money on soil. This can start to make the system feel pricier than traditional gardening systems.

However, there is a way around this. You can cover the bottom of your beds with twigs, wood chippings, and sawdust. Not only will these materials help to raise the beds, but they are also biodegradable. As such, they will break down over time and add more nutrients to the soil, while also saving you some money.

9. Refresh, nurture, and rotate your garden beds: The soil used in your square foot garden needs to be retouched yearly if it is to keep producing healthy plants. Add more manure, compost, and peat moss (optional) to replenish the nutrients used by your plants during the growing cycle.

Additionally, rotating your plants within the beds can help to reduce nutrient degradation as plants task the soil differently.

10. Treated scrap wood: The ideal wood for creating garden beds is the untreated variety. However, in the case that it is unavailable, you can use treated scrapwood. Just ensure that the wood isn't from any later than 2003. Any such material contains carcinogens which can transfer into the soil and plants, making both the medium and yield unsafe for consumption.

Cedar is one of the best kinds of wood to use for their purpose. It can last as long as 10 to 15 years, and that's without taking its inherent aesthetics into consideration. Keep in mind, though, that cedar tends to be quite expensive in certain areas. Whatever the case, look for a wood variety that is resistant to rot and is safe for plants and soil in the long run.

11. Think about the height: As mentioned earlier, there are plants that take up a lot of space in the garden but that are especially great for gardens that use vertical spaces. Plants that grow up help you better utilize space in square foot gardens. Since they are taller, they can be used to your advantage with the right planting layout.

For instance, there are plants that thrive better in heat. In such a case, to ensure better sunlight and warmth for those plants, try planting the taller crops on the north side of the garden bed. On the other hand, for plants that prefer shade and do not require direct access to sunlight, the taller plants can be grown in the middle of the garden bed.

By doing this, the plants that prefer the sun can be placed on the north side and get their fill of sunlight, and the plants that prefer shade will be saved by the tall plants overshadowing them.

12. Make use of a seeding square: Crops grown in square foot gardens are planted in spacings of 1, 4, 9, or 16. Vegetables take up to about four large squares. To ensure the correct spacing, you should use a planting tool called a seeding square.

This instrument helps you to accurately place the plants in the different squares with the recommended space for them to grow in a 1-foot square. Using it will allow you to make the most of your garden beds without overcrowding the growing medium or plants.

Chapter 9: How to Protect Your Square Foot Garden

The square foot garden system isn't without its fair share of inhibitions. Several phenomena, including pests and the weather, tend to affect plants from growing as well as you would hope. As such, it's imperative that allowances are made to properly deal with them within the growing cycle. Below are some methods to protect your square foot garden.

U-Frame Cages

To protect your beds and plants, start by making a U-frame cage that fits over your square bed. It's advisable to make U-frames of many different sizes to aptly deal with issues concerning one, two, or four square feet. Also, create one that can encompass an entire 4x4 box of 16 square feet. The idea is to make wire cages that can fit over the top of the aforementioned areas. Over time, you can add any covering made with a suitable material to protect the framed squares from potential hazards like pests and weather.

Experience has shown that the easiest materials to use for U-frames are wire fences coated in plastic. They can be easily cut into the desired sizes with pliers and can be bent in any shape across a straight edge. With two U-frames, you can make a two-sided or four-sided wire box for your garden beds. These plastic-coated wire fences come in several varieties with diverse lengths and breadths, as well as different wire thicknesses and openings.

Chicken Wire

Alternatively, you can use chicken wire which is an easy material to obtain. It comes with openings measuring between one and two inches. The 1-inch variety is the stronger of the two, although that extra durability comes at a higher price than the 2-inch variety. Furthermore, the durability makes the 1-inch size tougher to bend into shape, but the tinier openings mean it keeps more critters at bay than the 2-inch variety.

With a pair of cutting shears or pliers, you can cut chicken wire into any desired shapes and sizes. A whole roll of it can measure anywhere between three to four feet widthwise, but you can get even longer rolls from hardware stores.

Full Cages

Using chicken wire cages on your garden beds can help protect your crops from pests like birds and rabbits that dig up and feast on newly planted seeds. Cats also like to dig into the soil which can be bad for plants. Extensive exposure to the sun during the tender and delicate periods of the growing cycle can be detrimental to seedlings. The same applies to strong gusts of winds during the windy seasons. In this light, it's logical to build wire cages that fit the expected sizes of your plants at maturity.

It becomes rather difficult to take off the cages when the plants begin growing through them. This is especially so for creepers. With a full cage, you can interlace your fingers into the wire and pull it off to tend to your plants and replace it when you are done. Full cages work better with supports, usually wooden-frame bottoms, which are a perfect fit for wooden garden bed frames.

Chapter 10: Gardening Tips

What comes to your mind when you think of gardening? Fresh fruits and vegetables, perhaps, but also a lot of hard work, right? Well, if that's the case, here are 33 tips that can transform your gardening experience and make it both fun and productive!

1. **Know what to grow**: Whether you are planting a garden to save some money, to have a fresh supply of in-season vegetables, or simply because you think homegrown vegetables taste better, it is important to know exactly what you want to grow and how compatible the crops are with your soil. Finally, it is best to plant crops that are in season.

2. **Know what not to grow:** Knowing what not to plant in your garden is as important as knowing what to plant. There is no point in planting crops that you do not eat. Also avoid plants that are not compatible with your soil and that are difficult to cultivate, especially if you do not plan on doing gardening full time.

3. **Choose your location carefully**: Pick a location that has easy access to water and is well lit. Avoid areas with large trees or shrubs that could compete with your crops for sunlight, as light and water are very basic to the success of your crops. Also, choose rich, fertile, and well-

drained soil. In addition to that, your garden should be situated somewhere you can easily access. This way, you won't forget to tend to it.

4. **Choosing your beds**: Garden beds are essentially as important to the crops as the soil itself. Various types of garden beds are best suited for different types of crops, from in-ground beds to raised beds to containers.

5. **In-ground beds**: In-ground beds are dug directly in the ground at the same level as the soil surface; usually, the soil surface is not significantly higher than that of the surrounding areas. In-ground beds are probably the easiest to set up and require little or no raw materials to create.

6. **Raised beds**: The raised bed is basically an in-ground bed, but with its edges raised. This allows the soil to be built up. Similarly, a better soil type could be brought in and added to the already existing soil. When constructing a raised bed, it is important to avoid using railroad ties or pressure-treated woods as they contain materials that are toxic to both humans and crops.

7. **Containers**: Containers of various sizes are great for people with little to no space for gardening. Herbs such as

basil and thyme don't mind growing in pots at all, and you can always find a conducive spot for them.

8. **Invest in basic gardening tools**: Good gardening tools can make your job a lot easier, and they won't break under pressure. The importance of investing in quality gardening tools cannot be overemphasized. Imagine a scenario where your tool breaks in the middle of work, and you either have to stop work and head over to the store or put off the work immediately. No one wants to be placed in such a situation, so it is important to purchase not just the right tools but also quality ones.

9. **Get your soil tested**: Most people make the mistake of thinking they know their soil well merely by looking at it or by observing what sort of crops grow well in it. While it is good to study your soil and know what flourishes in it, you must not fail to test your soil before setting up your garden. A soil test helps you detect nutrient deficiencies, soil acidity, soil texture, and the percentage of organic matter present in the soil. This helps you improve your soil and make better choices when it comes to what crops you will plant in your garden. Soil testing, however, does not detect insufficient sunlight, poor drainage, or activities of insects and disease.

10. **Improve your soil**: As a gardener, improving your soil in order to maximize production and crop yield should be of utmost priority. Feeding your soil organic matter helps improve its overall quality, supplies crops with nutrients, and improves the soil structure. Supply what is missing in your soil, and don't forget to get in as much nitrogen as you can. Avoid harmful practices like planting the same crops every year. Rather, practice crop rotation every now and then. Growing cover crops is another way to improve the quality of your soil as they help prevent erosion and your soil from compacting.

11. **Choose your seeds with care**: Bad seeds are synonymous with a bad harvest. It's important to use seeds of good quality if you want your crops to grow strong, healthy, and able to resist disease and drought. In addition, good seeds respond well to fertilizers, leading to a better crop yield.

12. **Potting**: From wooden barrels to buckets, baskets, or just about anything that can hold soil, potting is an amazing way to plant a garden, especially if you're constrained by space. The only downside is that crops grown by potting will require some extra watering, often twice daily, to avoid drying out.

13. **How to select pots**: Clay pots are usually more attractive than plastic pots, but plastic pots hold moisture a lot better than the clay varieties. However, you can place a plastic pot inside a clay one to get both effects. Always remember that the larger the pot, the better. Crops need space to grow, so the more space you have in a pot, the more crops you can grow in it.

14. **Crop rotation**: This is simply the act of changing the position of various crops and vegetables in the garden over time. By rotating crops from one part of the garden to the other, you can help sustain and even boost soil nutrients. For example, you can plant shallow-rooted crops after deep-rooted crops and vice versa.

    Here is a sample plan for crop rotation in a garden:

	Site 1	Site 2	Site 3
1st year	A	B	C
2nd year	B	C	A
3rd year	C	A	B

15. **Invest in marigolds**: A common hand-me-down tradition among gardeners is investing in marigolds. These are typically planted next to tomatoes and help to

stave off common pests. While it remains to be proven whether or not marigold acts as an organic pesticide to tomato pests, it doesn't hurt to give it a try, and for all it's worth, it adds more beauty and color to your garden setup.

16. **Save some beer for your slug friends**: Slugs are a natural enemy to every gardener and can contribute to poor harvests in a growing season. However, as much as they are invested in ruining your plants for the sake of their tiny bellies, they enjoy a good beer, too. So, appeal to this bacchanalian side of these pests by putting out a shallow dish of stale beer, and watch them frolic to their deaths.

17. **Try soap shavings**: While it could easily be an old wives' tale, it's a popular belief that soap shavings help to repel animal pests like deer. So, to combat a deer problem in your garden, you might as well attempt this hack. Try spreading the shavings around the plants you wish to protect, and observe if it helps keep the deer at bay.

18. **Create your own insecticides**: Instead of investing in commercially-produced insecticides, you can create your own with trusted ingredients and that have less harmful effects on your plants in the long run. To make an insecticide, pour a tablespoon of liquid soap into one

gallon of water. Mix it thoroughly, and then pour the mixture into spray bottles. Spraying this on the stems and leaves of the affected plants can help combat pests such as spider mites and aphids. Make sure you reapply the solution after it rains.

19. **Bugs are your friends**: Bugs aren't always the enemy. In fact, they are good garden allies when they are eating the actual pests. As such, discovering techniques for using the good bugs to your advantage is a strategy practiced by many gardeners. This isn't exactly rocket science and can be achieved by planting certain kinds of herbs and flowers that attract the beneficial bugs like wasps, butterflies, and bees. These insects, in turn, help control other bug pests such as beetles and aphids.

20. **Don't be a perfectionist**: The rows of your garden beds need not be straight. If anything, do not be concerned about making perfectly straight rows, because when the rows are crooked, you have the chance to squeeze in a couple more plants around them without impeding the space of other crops. Square foot gardening can help with this technique as you can make the most of square-foot areas to maximize the yield in less space.

21. **Practice picking off pests**: There are many tips and tricks online for dealing with garden pests. However,

sometimes, it falls to you to pick pests off your plants with your hands. This technique is especially useful for dealing with pests like squash bugs and Japanese beetles. Picking them off and dropping them into a bucket of soapy water is all you need to do. Sure, it's a time-consuming method and backbreaking work, but it's arguably the best solution yet. Also, observing your ants regularly and watching out to ward off problematic bugs before they multiply is vital.

22. **Water your plants in the morning**: It's inconceivable that this tip even exists, but you'd be surprised at how many people fail to follow such a simple rule. The most effective time to water your plants is in the morning since less moisture is likely to evaporate due to heat. Make this tip a priority for your plants, and watch your garden bloom.

23. **New plants need all the water they can get**: Germination is no easy process, and new plants require more help than others to establish and fend for themselves. As such, it's important to water them often. This tip is also applicable to trees. Watering them thoroughly during the first year of their growing cycle helps them grow deeper and thicker roots.

24. **Plan your garden according to the weather**: Remember the passage, "He who considers the weather

shall not sow/reap"? Well, forget it. Throughout the ages, gardeners have always kept an eye out for the weather, and you should do no differently. If you want to add compost or fertilizers to your garden, the best time to do that is just before the rains come. Also, the best time for planting is overcast days as there isn't a lot of wind. Ensure you monitor the weather forecast for each week and use it as a planning guide for your garden activities.

25. **Repurpose your kitchen scraps as compost**: Back in the day, gardeners used to dig holes around the edges of gardens and bury kitchen scraps. This old-fashioned method of composting requires no composter and works just as good in modern times. Even better is the fact that food waste creates great natural nutrients that plants can feed on.

26. **Throw in some eggshells**: Another age-old life hack used by gardeners is crushed eggshells. When utilized within your garden, expect to grow healthier and bigger plants. No rigamarole is involved. Simply ground up the eggshells and scatter them around the root base of your plants. Alternatively, you can add them as another constituent of your compost pile.

27. **Mulch, mulch, and mulch some more**: Straw, organic mulch, and wood chips are some materials that

help reintroduce nutrients back into the soil naturally. Additionally, mulching helps with the water retention of the soil, further helping to keep soil temperature manageable and prevent the growth of weeds. Put simply, mulching is one of the most cost-effective and intelligent ways to ensure that your garden soil remains good and productive in both the short and long-term.

28. **Save your seeds**: One of the cheapest ways to maintain your garden is to plant open-pollinated crops using their seeds instead of purchasing the seedlings of hybrid plants. To do this, you will have to save those seeds over the period of a year or more. This tip doesn't work for hybrid plants which you can neither save nor regrow seeds from. With this technique, you should be able to grow a complete food garden for many years without having to spend anything. Additionally, you should consider swapping seeds to help improve the variety in your garden without the need for investment.

29. **Invest in recycled seedling containers**: When you start planting your seeds in the spring, don't invest valuable funds on getting store-bought seedling pots. You can easily turn many of your household items into the perfect temporary home for your little plants. You can use a variety of things for your seeds, ranging from yogurt cups to toilet paper rolls to berry containers to eggshells.

Berry containers can serve as miniature greenhouses, as well.

30. **Repurpose empty milk containers**: There are many uses for milk jugs in the garden. For instance, they can be used as miniature greenhouses for seedlings, flower pots, birdseed scoops, watering cans, and other things. They can also serve as protection against the elements. By cutting off the base part of an empty jug, you can place the top over your seedlings to shield them from cool temperatures, heavy rains, hail, and wind.

31. **Try overwintering your annual crops**: This technique combines money-saving and climate control. By overwintering your annual crops, you can help them survive indoors away from the harsh winter weather. There is nothing to lose, so it's perfectly safe to try. All you need to do is dig up the entire plant, roots, and shoot. However, it's important to be careful when handling the stems to prevent breaking them. Transfer the plant into a pot that's specially curated with layers of compost and potting mix. Ensure that the new medium has good drainage. With this technique, you will be able to get some annual crops like pansies and geraniums to continue growing until they are replanted in the garden when spring comes.

32. **Be a cheerful giver**: Many perennial crops benefit from getting divided every couple of years. This is also a good way to share your crops with friends and family. Plants such as phlox, black-eyed Susans, coneflowers, daisies, daylilies, and other perennial crops can be split and shared with friends. The remaining part of the plant tends to grow stronger and healthier. For vegetables, you can save the seeds and disperse them among your friends.

33. **Plants can be hand-me-downs**: There is a different kind of feeling that comes with planting seeds that are from your parents or grandparents. The same feeling comes with the task of keeping a houseplant alive that is over 50 years old. When plants are handed down from one generation to the other, it improves the garden benefits already seen. Also, it further helps in connecting you to family, friends, and the generations before you.

Conclusion

Gardening might be a hobby for you, or a means of livelihood. Either way, you should be more enlightened about what square foot gardening entails and its benefits after having read this book.

To afford you a more thorough appreciation for square foot gardening, this book went into detail about its history and a very important part of its effectiveness: companion planting.

Hopefully, you have read this book with intention and will begin to put the knowledge you have gained into practice. For beginner gardeners, please know that some creativity will be required of you to get the most out of your square foot garden and companion planting. This creativity is the result of practical application and experience.

If you love and enjoy the process of growth, you will be rewarded with the beauty and fruits of nature!

CPSIA information can be obtained
at www.ICGtesting.com
Printed in the USA
BVHW041804281121
622723BV00027B/911